DOOM SCROLL

MATTHEW GUENETTE

 The University of Akron Press
Akron, Ohio

ISBN: 978-1-62922-231-8 (paper)
ISBN: 978-1-62922-232-5 (ePDF)
ISBN: 978-1-62922-233-2 (ePub)

A catalog record for this title is available from the Library of Congress.

∞ The paper used in this publication meets the minimum requirements of
ANSI/NISO z39.48–1992 (Permanence of Paper).

Cover: Photo of water: Ali Abdul Rahman, courtesy of Unsplash.com. Cover
design by Amy Freels and Thea Ledendecker.

Doom Scroll was designed and typeset in Minion with Futura titles by Amy
Freels and printed on sixty-pound natural and bound by Baker & Taylor
Publisher Services of Ashland, Ohio.

Produced in conjunction with the
University of Akron Affordable
Learning Initiative. More information
is available at
www.uakron.edu/affordablelearning/

DOOM SCROLL

AKRON SERIES IN POETRY

AKRON SERIES IN POETRY
Mary Biddinger, Editor

Emilia Phillips, *Signaletics*
John Repp, *Fat Jersey Blues*
Oliver de la Paz, *Post Subject: A Fable*
Brittany Cavallaro, *Girl-King*
Jennifer Moore, *The Veronica Maneuver*
Philip Metres, *Pictures at an Exhibition: A Petersburg Album*
Emilia Phillips, *Groundspeed*
Leslie Harrison, *The Book of Endings*
Sandra Simonds, *Further Problems with Pleasure*
Matthew Guenette, *Vasectomania*
Aimée Baker, *Doe*
Anne Barngrover, *Brazen Creature*
Emilia Phillips, *Empty Clip*
Emily Rosko, *Weather Inventions*
Caryl Pagel, *Twice Told*
Tyler Mills, *Hawk Parable*
Brittany Cavallaro, *Unhistorical*
Krystal Languell, *Quite Apart*
Oliver de la Paz, *The Boy in the Labyrinth*
Joshua Harmon, *The Soft Path*
Kimberly Quiogue Andrews, *A Brief History of Fruit*
Emily Corwin, *Sensorium*
Annah Browning, *Witch Doctrine*
Sean Shearer, *Red Lemons*
Heather Green, *No Other Rome*
Jennifer Moore, *Easy Does It*
Emilia Phillips, *Embouchure*
Aimee Seu, *Velvet Hounds*
Charles Jensen, *Instructions between Takeoff and Landing*
Heathen, *Outskirts*
Caryl Pagel, *Free Clean Fill Dirt*
Matthew Guenette, *Doom Scroll*

Titles published since 2013.
For a complete listing of titles published in the series,
go to www.uakron.edu/uapress/poetry.

CONTENTS

Love Will Tear Us Apart

You're a forty, no fifty-something Gen Xer and a former latchkey kid.

You have the privilege of a mortgage. You've mortgaged the future with your privilege. There are at least six different kinds of jellies in your fridge.

It's confusing, all this ordinary extraordinary.

All this supervision.

You've kicked your kids off the computers and TV and made them listen to Joy Division. You're waiting for them to get bored enough to play a board game or have a conversation.

You move the upstairs bedroom to the downstairs bedroom and the downstairs bedroom to the curb.

The sun is trying to come out but so is the moon, so are cicadas, so is the lightning.

There are rocks your kids throw into a lake and there are rocks the lake slowly throws back.

At the feeder, a hummingbird
bullies another hummingbird—

You can't get over it, the
comedy and tragedy of hummingbird
politics wrapped in the beauty of
hummingbirds.

Sticky Notes

: You can hear the stopwatch. The
authorities say you're out of timeouts.

    A to-do list of sticky notes
rises like little yellow suns—

    *Avoid the strip search, scoop the
cat box, stay away from the valley (it's
on fire!), call someone about the brakes,
call your mother* (who's been dead now
twenty years), etc.

    When you're awake your mind
is a tongue—

    It folds in on itself.

    You need help.

    If you're free, it's because you
have no problem not getting anything
done.

Worst Punk Band

: I practiced, but never got past just burning through chords like a backup in the worst punk band.

How does anyone rest?

According to the shingles, my roof is either weathered or sun-kissed, but the real black hole is binary thinking, especially for stars.

A drone chased its reflection into my windows and died beautifully in the artificial flowers.

Never check beneath the stalls; it's poor etiquette.

The bad haircuts I gave myself as a kid prepared me for the bad haircuts that adults would give me.

Someone stole my bike. Quickly I figured out it was a bicycle thief.

I had this friend in junior high. He was a real daredevil. When bored he would light, for instance, a paper airplane and sail it burning over a history lesson. If a teacher threatened to call his mom, he'd say: *Hell no, I'm going to call your mom.*

I thought that was excellent. I keep paying for that thought.

Awesome Dad

: You'd be surprised at how emotional he gets at baby pictures or predictions of extinction-level events.

Of course, Awesome Dad will buy the damned scrunchies! Of course, he'll forget everything he's said.

When he clogs the toilet again, he won't need your micro aggressive sympathy. He'll need $50,000 in cash to crash into his head.

The fossils he pretends to find when he digs a hole in the yard. The black box from a famous wreck. On behalf of his kids, he'll watch a sitcom about an idiot rich family and their jackass nanny, and he won't complain about wanting to die.

When love comes undone like a shoelace, Awesome Dad may inspire a crisis of trust. He might drop a few thousand f-bombs while he wrestles with the directions.

It makes no sense, the everything he wants, the way everything splinters.

In search of a perfect tomato, he daydreams of a coconut packed with cocaine.

He puts his Awesome Dad shoulder to the wheel, saves receipts, tapes the kids' artwork over a desk.

He will ask, and not always half-heartedly, if anyone needs help.

Cul-de-Sac

: Every night I was eviscerated, a nuclear strike parachuting down—these were my nightmares in the '80s.

The inevitable late summer light that fills me with an exquisite melancholy.

My friend who became a cop and my friend who went to prison grew up in the same cul-de-sac.

I wouldn't want to live in a cul-de-sac's fallacy of circular reasoning.

The therapist I saw wondered what I feared more, boredom or death or spammers calling about expired car warranties.

The simple, satisfying bread I can bake. The easy way I'm distracted or mistrust myself.

First, I read books to help me understand my father. He always hired the same handyman whose face had been disfigured in an accident. Then I read books to help me be a father.

There's an equation I can't make sense of.

Eventually I quit wiping my nose on my sleeve. Eventually I got hired at a restaurant where I bussed tables either high or extremely hungover. To the fry cook who would always ask, I'd say, *I'm doing good.*

To which he would reply, with authority, *You mean you're doing well.*

Rubber Chicken

: I'm in New Hampshire somewhere,
in a Denny's actually.

The meal is totally adequate.
The news I'm reading however, about
a woman who attacks another with
a spatula, is amazing. The attack gets
thwarted when the victim fights back
with a rubber chicken.

You never know when you'll
need a rubber chicken.

You never know when you'll
have to dig up your father's grave to
revive an argument the two of you
had been having your whole life. In
that news, the arresting officer says
the suspect seemed drunk. And
was quoting from the Bible when
confronted.

When I look up from my plate,
it's the hottest summer on record. I
notice a red and pink rhododendron
in a planter outside. You never know
when you'll notice the rhododendron
and want to fall to your knees. Which
is why whenever I'm at a Denny's, I
long for New Hampshire.

Motivational Poster

: The impulse moves at the speed of an impulse.

The galaxy obscured by its dust. Trick questions obscured by punctuation.

The poster outside my cubicle—
It's a two-dimensional impression of depth, height, width, a.k.a. "the plane of focus."

It's meant to be motivational, but how?

Space-time bends around a spreadsheet.

The red message light on my phone blinks its irritated eye.

Should anyone think to come get me, they'll see the sticky notes on my desk arranged in an SOS.

Punk Song

My daughter worried the milk had spoiled because her brother left it out, but I was worried the kids were spoiled.

Was the milk out for an hour, or was it fine five minutes ago?

The kids were smart and sophisticated enough to want to play in the woods, so that's where we would go, but we would have to cross some busy streets first.

You never know if all those drivers have accident-free records; that's the thrill of crossing a street, but before we look both ways, we must remember to look both ways.

When I told my kids that anxiety is simply a dump of chemicals putting your prefrontal cortex on hold while your emotions take over, it really freaked them out.

They asked about sword fighting with sticks. But what happens if the sword fighting gets out of hand? What if someone loses an eye on the rusty fence near the rickety slide and that used needle in the park?

I wanted my kids to banish those thoughts like those French fries someone threw.

We were almost to the woods—

The woods dark with feelings, dark with trails winding through the undergrowth. The trails dividing into more trails. The undergrowth where when the wind blows it sounds like heavy breathing extremely nearby.

But what if we get lost? they asked.

Seriously, I said, *I'm lost already.*

Finger Roll

: The problem is I'm older than
Nintendo 64—that's how my kids put
it—
     I had an easy breakaway,
nothing guarding me but air and sky
for that George Gervin finger roll, but
there was my knee, folding like the
lawn chair I sat in last summer.

I have what's left of a meniscus after it
flips like a bucket handle. I have a disc
in my back that on an MRI looks like
meat jerked from a lobster claw.

When my father was dying, he got
anxious and poetic, practiced his
senses. He wanted me to know he'd
wrestled many bar stools when the
moon was up—
     Sometimes he lost, sometimes
he won, either way it was a good run.

When I get on the floor to stretch,
I grunt like Bigfoot, hope for
improvement, vow to be no hoax—
     That American dad who buys
a Corvette to match the little dragon
tattoo breathing fire down his back.

Eventually I took the kids to the park.
We stomped the wood chips, got high
on the monkey bars. I even managed
a few chin-ups with a look on my face
that said this hurts way less than it
hurts.

Lurid Dreamcatcher

: It's like a test. I watch a wife put her husband in a headlock and snake him across the lawn. Another neighbor pours chemicals over their flowers to make them laugh louder.

I can hear someone shouting somewhere about something. The shouts mix with the dusk.

The flowers answer by laughing louder.

My neighbor's wind chime made of beer cans.

The unexpected underwear draped over a fence like a lurid dreamcatcher.

Some kids on bikes playing demolition derby in the hell strip.

Do I mostly wear clothes when I wander the yard? Of course! How clueless do you think I am?

Then I drag our perfectly trashed trashcans to the curb, and make sure the lids are secured so the raccoons won't climb in and start the end of the world.

Put It on a T-Shirt

: Your neighbor in the MAGA hat has answers. He lets you borrow his tools. His bird feeder and yours get raided by the same squirrels. How about that for a country song?

You imagine a future where the important questions that unfold might go something like this—Is Jesus king, or is science king, or is Budweiser king?

Death by a thousand paperless billing paper cuts.

You keep checking the news to see who's been captured and who's winning. You keep forgetting to invent a TikTok dance or whatever your destiny is.

You're pretty sure, though, that the arguments your neighbors' lawn signs are having will outlive the lawns.

You're pretty sure we shouldn't be so annoyed at the squirrels for their perfectly American desires. *Put it on a T-shirt*, your neighbor says. On this point, you agree.

Pigeon

: A man at the bagel shop wore a sweatshirt. It had an American flag sort of dragon-type thing on it unplayfully clawing its way through the slogan: *If This Offends You, I'll Help You Pack.*

If only I'd been wearing a sweatshirt that said: *If the Offense I Take at the Innumerable Offenses of Our Country Offends You, I'll Help You Pack.*

I've read about folks who've seen flying saucers. I knew this guy— he looked me right in the eye and swore a shadowy half-man, half-bird creature was creeping through ditches alongside Midwestern interstates.

When my kids are older, what will be the facts? Will they be able to order bullets with their bagels and coffee?

Have I ever known how to feel?

Sometimes F-35s use the airport by the college. You can never tell whether they're taking off or coming in—they move that fast.

When you look up, maybe the sky is overcast. It sounds like the world is tearing in half but all you see is a pigeon swoop low from a wire.

Shipwreck

: My kids wanted to know where babies come from. The dining room table was littered with the following: scissors, Cheerios, sticky notes, a spider made of pipe cleaners and, on someone's science homework, a half-drawn cartoon of a farting teacher. *Is it dangerous*, they asked, *the moon, a river, or if you stick your tongue to a 9-volt battery?* The tongue is an excellent conductor of electricity, but I wasn't ready to go there. Then the kids said we should get a bass so they could start a punk band, a fantastic idea, yes, yet already I could see it, the bass alone in its corner, the ideas for a band extremely un-furthered. The kids insisted I watch while they attempted to lick their elbows. They swore that "frig" was not a swear, no matter what the librarian said. My friend told me that when she asked her mom where babies come from, what she described sounded more like a shipwreck of question marks than sex. Then a story came on the radio about the latest school shooter. The kids wanted to know why that happened, why that man did what he did. I was afraid to guess, and I stayed that way, until the kids got distracted by an old cheetah print onesie and tried to put it on the cat.

Your Results Aren't Good

: I liked the meadow better when
McMansions didn't surround it—

The eye doctor says, *Your results aren't
good.* The patient asks, *Could I see
them?* The eye doctor says, *Probably
not.*

The leader of the free world, in an
effort to educate everyone on the
importance of the arts in uncertain
times, gets on Twitter and calls the
experts a thankless gang of losers.

First there were fields, then there were
soccer fields, then there were bleachers
where any curious adult could sit
and watch a confused kid like me
accidently score on their own goal.

I, Too, Have Been Unfaithful

: What about the *thermo*nuclear family? Your dad threatening meltdown over a clogged toilet or an oil puddle in the drive?

Yes, when the weather's nice, you can see Jesus on his porch. He's sipping whiskey. He's got something in his beard. He's working on his zombie novel to heal his wounds.

Charlie Brown is a porn star *and* a Marxist—
      (That's what the graffiti at the bus stop said.)

I, too, have been unfaithful. All it takes is a field of dandelions to break me in half.

Thank god, though, for time—
      (It keeps everything from happening at once.)

Chicken Sandwich

: When I lived in the basement apartment, a blue-haired punker lived upstairs. One night she brought me a chicken sandwich. *Bon appétit,* she said. Then we ended up fooling around. Her dog puked in my shoes. She was studying to be a scientist so she would say things like *There's a bacterium that uses arsenic in place of phosphorus in its DNA,* which I loved but only understood euphemistically. She put me to work. Our experiments, so to speak, lasted a month, until her boyfriend found out about me and my girlfriend found out about her. Eventually, conveniently, my apartment flooded.

Middle School Research Project

: A man retreated to a cave with his children. All of them died when he detonated the suicide vest. *Being in school is like being in prison*, my son said with a totally straight face. By the dark of November, I tried to agree— *Yes*, I said, *ideas can trap us; it's easier sometimes just to sleep.* Vulnerability is a kind of freedom too but try explaining that to a teenager. When my son said dreams send us the past, I was impressed. He had been having this recurring one about an endless swing set where he desperately ducks. It reminded me of a dream from my own childhood; it took place in a warehouse from the corners of which rolled gigantic metal spheres I had to outrun. My son did his middle school research project, he tried—he figured out there were experts who believed some things were real, and there were experts who believed those other experts were fake.

Seasons of Mists
and Mellow Fruitfulness

: Snoop Dogg says read the syllabus. It's heavy.

Your conspiracy theorist called; he wants you to know he's sloshed and still lives with his mom.

Every day, seasons of mists and mellow fruitfulness and the Mega Millions jackpots keep getting bigger.

Am I the only one who wonders what Bigfoot wonders about what the anti-vaxxers wonder about cryptozoologists?

Someone dressed like the Statue of Liberty twirls a sign outside the shady tax office.

Perfect circles drawn around perfect circles on a paper spinning on a turn table—

My kids are watching this and various other dreamed up things on YouTube. They assure me it's all part of the job.

Space Smells Like Metal

: He knew he should be grateful, and so reminded himself to pay attention to the trees, but it was dark, he couldn't really see them, could only hear them in the breeze. It sounded good, like waves at the shore, a lesson for how important it is to stay flexible, even though he had trouble touching his toes. He considered the darkness, which quickly raised thoughts of his bank account; the balance was dangerously low. He thought of a friend of a friend who fell through a roof and broke their hip; it was a miracle—not the broken hip part, the part where they weren't paralyzed or dead—and he remembered too his son had worried about getting sick from a computer that had been infected with a virus. His son had read somewhere that astronauts claim space smells like metal and seared steak, which sounds terrifying, but he thought of space nevertheless, that dark oscillating mass, and of the lights which dim through it. One of those lights turned out to be a TV some neighbors had moved to their garage and plugged in to a generator. That's where they were, eating dinner and laughing and watching the game, trying to answer the dark.

Credit Card

I try to cancel my credit card.

While I'm put on hold, I imagine every megachurch along I-35, from Duluth to Laredo, broadcasting my Social Security number on a large technological display as part of some watered-down liturgy on psychology, patriotism, and fundraising.

I've been told that Jesus, who never got married or held a steady job or kept a permanent address, would like me to carry on in his image.

I've been told Jesus, who was sure his mother was a virgin and who never had to empty the trash or mow a lawn, means to point me in the direction of the lowest, most competitive rates.

What could be more biblical than, say, a debt, which is nothing more than a coercion, a predicament, symptomatic of some issue that presumes upon the future like a boss who thinks he knows everything?

What could be more biblical than, say, unspecified charges, charged without my consent, that take thirty-three years to pay down?

If it could, my credit score would ding so loud they would name a five-alarm chili after me in Oklahoma City, a place where the cost of living is low, gas is cheap, and where I felt like a pebble dropped in a lake when, in a bar surrounded by cowboys and sunburnt suburbs and blistered fields, someone stole my wallet.

I Against I

The middle-aged men I knew growing up—

Their beer bellies made them look pregnant with beer, their lives made me buy that Bad Brains record.

What if I wore a bandana and jumped out of a plane? What if Bad Brains had sung about the audacity of listening to Top 40 while picking up your kids from school in a minivan full of groceries—

Who would have listened?

The first flip phones were almost as smart as dogs. The new toasters look like miniature megachurches. Chicken sandwiches taking over the world, love songs lying about love taking over the radio, paranoid delusions taking over your mid-life crisis.

Did you get the memo? Do you remember that arrogant punker from school who wore spiked belts and a green mohawk? He sincerely tried to warn us. *One day*, he said, *you'll be a cautionary tale for your kids.*

I Used to Be a Landscaper

: That's just another way of saying I used to cut grass and whip weeds for minimum wage. Everybody knows this.

Petroleum transfer engineers still existed when I was a kid; they would pump your gas at the gas station. The educational nourishment consultants would spoon sloppy joes in your school cafeteria. A domestic technician would shout at you to clean your room.

My boss—I want to say my horrible boss—would ask me to do things like load 300-pound water tanks on a truck while he and the "senior landscaper" sat in the air-conditioned office smoking cigars and playing cards.

One morning he said I needed to go down to where the millionaires lived, on a road by the beach. There was a mansion there with a turf problem. I was to roll up the turf, collect the fat white grubs from underneath and drop them in a coffee can filled with gasoline, then roll the turf back out. This was to be done as a favor for my boss, who would have it done as favor for his millionaire brother-in-law.

Because I already had poison ivy and sunburn and a sprained back from those water tanks, I sighed.

My boss never missed a chance to launch into a lecture about hard work and earning your keep. He said I needed to learn about life, that it's a bull you must grab by the horns. I thought that sounded stupid, and I said so, like something an idiot does just before they're ground into a paste.

A Wicked Case of Hiccups

: We probably need milk and coffee if the family is to survive. We probably need more time to feel less lost about how little time there is to be found. I had a wicked case of hiccups, but a wickeder case of existential crisis. The cosmos had misaligned like a senator's spine. My neighbor wasn't happy either; I still had his extension ladder and neither of us knew why. I was caught in a time loop. There was a time loop I was caught in. The time loop had caught me. Later, trying to get serious at work, I entered the password with the best of intentions, but the computer kept saying *wrong, wrong, wrong*. When I tried to reset it, the computer said the new password can't be the old password. It occurred to me I was hungry. It occurred to me that maybe I should set fire to the place, break a few windows at least, but I was working from home. At some point I felt the stabbing pains. All the best laid plans, I kept tripping over them, with no idea who left them out.

Wormhole

: It was fun for a minute, having no idea what day it was. Was it time to jump online or mask up for groceries? The kids sighed, forced themselves to finish their history and math.

Time was like some weirdo in their pajamas in the middle of the afternoon while the moon is still out, grinding a skateboard on your curb, taking selfies in front of your house with your face in the window.

One night I noticed the lamplight inch along gravity's curved path.

I imagined a wormhole had sprung between the TV and the couch. It was funny—or was it?

To have felt those infinite parts of yourself, those strings and loops doing what they do.

I remembered that joke about a clock with no numbers. It's a timeless joke. A joke about stars, etc., impossible odds, a lack of information...

Nuclear Volleyball

My wife and I stood there staring at the volleyball that had just landed between us. We were playing a friendly backyard game with our young neighbors, the Youngs, who had stepped away for a moment for some energy drinks.

Nuts! said my wife.

I said, *You think the Youngs have had butt lifts?*

Maybe we need a different ball, said my wife, *a nuclear volleyball, a volleyball made of fire.*

Crackers, the Youngs' young know-it-all parrot, perched on the net like a blue-and-gold referee

Nuts! it squawked. *Nuclear volleyball! Butt lifts!*

The Youngs, still drinking their energy drinks, high-fiving like they won the world...

Discount Hand Grenades

: On the Zoom call my brother offered condolences for the bowl of Fritos and chili cheese I was eating. He bragged about how he had made a salad. It even had nuts and berries in it. As if…

What my brother hadn't done was shave in over a month.

He said he was going for a look, Adirondack Taliban, and when our shared soul laughed, we weren't sure what to make of that, our thoughts, or the way we feel…

The shows we had binge-watched already were *Atlanta*, *BoJack Horseman*, and *Tiger King*. That Joe Exotic had run for governor was almost as crazy as the fact he'd snagged twenty percent of the vote.

If only we could save the world one tasteless joke at a time.

How would you like a bullet-hole tattoo right there over your heart? Should we head to Walmart for discount hand grenades?

Though he'd lost his job my brother felt lucky—that's what he said, *I truly feel lucky*—that no one we knew yet was alone in a room dying to breathe.

Then my brother said we should have our own show—we would don the masks, drag America into one of its lawless backyards, and challenge it to a fight.

Hazmat Suit

: My kids weren't the only ones misinformed by some numbnuts on TikTok.

There he is, in a hazmat suit, the numbnuts on TikTok. The hazmat suit proves he's an expert. His opinion proves the virus was made in a lab where they crossed a bullet with a bat.

My kids must be dragged from that deathly entertainment back into the present.

That thing about fate in the lines of your palm and a dial tone in your brain. That thing about washing your hands twenty seconds at a time for the rest of your life.

The future is where our descendants will speak from. They'll ask for advice. They'll wonder about our unfinished drywall and sunlamps and what it was like to work remotely in a shirt and tie with pajamas pants.

When we see, it's practically at the speed of light—that's the future.

Before I shut down for the night, I show my kids something good—how to make a meal with just a box of noodles, a can of diced tomatoes, and half an onion that's been sitting on the counter all week.

When I chop it up, it's just like in the old days. Everyone cries.

The Great Pyramids

: You travel to the great pyramids of toilet paper at Walmart.

You wear a mask.

It would be fascinating, you think, to see oil paintings of politicians getting fact-checked in real time on live TV.

In a dream, your arm is hooked up to something that resembles a pulsing squid, but it's just the secret to your mother's meatloaf the authorities are after.

You understand flash grenades will light up the streets like the Fourth of July even though it's not quite the Fourth of July.

Is history a series of reforms everyone must bang their heads against?

Does it require all the Walmart greeter's strength to smile in front of the display of tiny American flags?

You remember a game of Scrabble where you misspelled *mistake* as *misteak*. But you love steak.

You wonder when the protestors will set up tables where they can sell their homemade relish.

The great pyramid scheme continues to be built by the exact number of suckers born every minute. You reason that the mysterious void at its center is probably the tomb of an ancient scam.

You understand; it's not the heat but the heat wave.

It turns all the maps the exact blood red of your stepfather's power tie.

Bigger Wave

: Someone asks why you got the compass tattoo. You say to match the fish and lake tattoo, though it can feel like meaning can mean next to nothing or close to it sometimes.

When you jump-stop and go up strong it's not strong enough. Not nearly. Someone younger and faster comes along—it's scary how fast—and swats your shot to the fence.

A part of you thinks you can still steal away, start an over-forty punk band, scream songs that answer the important questions like, *Do you know how much these swim lessons will cost?*

You wonder how good you must be at anything. Then the kids want to go for a swim, which everyone loves, especially that part where you wade in and turn around and wave at everyone who loves you and a bigger wave flowers over your sunburned shoulders and knocks the glasses off your head.

If only the kids would laugh only at this for rest of your not-long-enough life.

When you snap a selfie with the ATM behind you, it looks like money wants to eat you alive.

You drive by Target and the word *tarjay* drifts though your mind like the whitest thought ever.

A dance you do in the kitchen is roughly the equivalent of Bon Jovi's hair circa "Livin' on a Prayer."

Your son comes in for an awkward high-five. Your daughter wants a magical rainbow pony. You tell them again about the time you nearly lost them at a festival to save the lakes. Here's what happened—

You turned around for just a minute to get everyone hot dogs and chips. And when you turned back, SNAP! just like that, they were gone.

You Sound Like Your Mother

: It's the words themselves that glitter and buzz, *that's* the story.

When those kids crashed their bikes into your trash bins, it sounded like the drums from "In the Air Tonight."

What kind of feeling is that, the ingenious genius who wants you to know invaluable things are valuable?

There's a way to say *beer can* so it sounds like *bacon*, but it doesn't work in reverse.

The doctor wants you to notice that sometimes you sound like your mother, especially when you're telling someone that they sound like their mother.

Sometimes a word bends a blade of grass. When that happens, look out.

This Guy from Turkey

—for Josh Bell

: I was playing chess online against this guy from Turkey. I don't know if he was a guy from Turkey. He just said he was a guy from Turkey.

He could've been some dude in his mother's basement in Indiana waiting for the apocalypse—You never know.

But I do know his screenname was *invincible*, and he was not invincible.

Not that I'm any good either.

I've lost thousands of games to players with screennames like *buttmilk* and *thundercheese2000*.

The best I ever played was a ten-year-old kid, in person, at some chess club that met at a McDonalds. I had to act like it didn't bother me while he slurped soda and picked through a mountain of fries and blitzed me into a mess.

If anyone asks, I say it was like getting beaten up by a teddy bear.

Anyway, here's what happened with *invincible*—When I put him in check, instead of saving his king or resigning, he logged off with too much time left on the clock.

If he was a guy from Turkey, he disappeared into fifteen million other lives and the mystery of Istanbul where you can walk from Asia to Europe and back while eating a Big Mac.

Once time ran out, the game declared, *You win by abandonment.*

I wondered what else could be won that way. Parenting? The lottery? My job?

Wouldn't that put more time on the big clock, the one no one can get their hands on?

Doom Scroll

: The curve flattens as shampoo gets in your eyes.

You sip a quarantini in your jammies.

Watch *Scrubs* reruns you'll never watch again.

Listen to an '80s mixtape.

A kind of Western plants itself in your dreams, and you remember—

A desert flowering red, some managerial-looking dudes riding donkeys.

The managerial-looking dudes all wear nametags. The nametags all say the same thing: *Hello, my name is Dick.*

A Quick Bedtime Story

: My daughter asked for a quick bedtime story. *Fine*, I said, *being is the horizon of time, now please go to sleep.*

When she said it might be the other way around, that time is the horizon of all being, I asked her how she knew that.

From experience, she said. *From experience...*

GO TEAM!

: A man sprouts mop-hair from his head. He's turning into a mascot.

Watch the mask bite his face.

Watch the furred red suit soak with sweat.

"GO TEAM!" he shouts as he drops the kids off at school. "GO TEAM!" he shouts as the automatic doors of the grocery store slide open.

It takes effort, in the furry oversized mascot gloves, to plug in a toaster or pay bills.

Yet when a stunt goes wrong, when a fly ball out of nowhere smacks him in the head, our mascot understands: his suit is no place to lose faith.

He wears it to bed, hoping a lover will get into it.

Soon everyone is wearing one—the kids' teachers and the automated grocery check-out and that insane person on the radio talking about what's wrong with the world.

The man in the mascot suit shouts, "GO TEAM!" There's a desk at work he jumps up on. There are invisible bars he pretends to get his head stuck in as he tries to squeeze free.

Is there no end to the unimportant documents he can slam dunk in the recycling bin?

Will we remember when he faceplants into a coworker that his springy antennae went "BOING!"

How will we hear "GO TEAM!" as denial or a kind of permission? while everyone follows him out to the parking lot where a ring of fire awaits the mascot in his extremely flammable polyester suit.

Jack and Diane

: We were in the yard, sunny for the first time that spring, almost seventy degrees, some dull-looking birds making a ruckus by the fence, probably over a ladybird, so I said, *Let's get dangerous, let's fool around in the honeysuckle, honey,* but she was like, *We should dig those shrubs up, they're invasive you know, and plant berries till this whole yard is nothing but fruit,* and I was like, *Or maybe we could go over there behind the shady tree, we could suck on chili dogs and if you put on Bobbie Brooks slacks, whatever the hell those are, you could dribble them off and we could do what we please,* and she was like, *Or maybe Danny would let us borrow his chainsaw, we could carve out the ash stump, plant geraniums and marigolds in there, a little temple of color,* and I was like, *But the weather's so nice, it's practically a sin, let's drink beer and get down,* and she was like, *You know what would really turn me on is if you raked those leaves* (those endless leaves) *and dragged them to the curb,* but she said it in such a sexy way, like the end of the world was nowhere in sight—there was no way I could say no.

Gutter Guy

: What the gutter guy does is put his mind in the gutter. He comes over, blows out the rotting leaves like bad memories.

We have a tree wizard too. He pumps a "treatment" in the ash, so borers won't crash it down into the death of me.

Anyone can see I'm trapped. I thrash in the honeysuckle, its twining vines succeeding when I land a gash in my thumb with the axe.

If only I could fix the fixtures. If only all those insider goons who ensure nothing good gets done would go do something else.

When the sky brightens, I'm blinded.

The opinionated blue jays are like talk show hosts. *Fat chance!* they jeer at our fat cat sunning himself near a bag of charcoal. The charcoal I left out in the rain.

A neighbor texts wondering what our daughter is allergic to as she, our daughter, raids a bag of their Funyuns.

I didn't know Funyuns were still legal.

Will the polar ice keep melting if my son leaves another wet towel on the floor?

How much longer will I live in this self, in this body that wants and wants

I sauté onions for the enchiladas no one wants me to make. Standing there in my old school Adidas and grass-stained jeans, spatula in one hand, flat beer in the other, I'm the dad my dad and I never had.

I have feelings like the bills I'll never pay off.

I have feelings like the warranties I dig up in the junk drawer that promise to take care of it all.

Din

: Din of my daughter's sleep-hair no
match for the comb.

Din of hairdryer and toothpaste,
promises we can or can't keep...

Din of weeds, of hydra-headed things
gone to seed in the yard though flowers
have nothing on dandelions.

Din of the "I" as proof of desire, of the
body that wants more and more.

Din of the dinner defrosting, of $1.31
vacuumed up in the cushions and the
din of what little we can do with it.

Din of stars.

Din of false starts...leaves in the slats,
an altar of tassels...

Din of stains that won't come out, of
the last rat's ass my friend said she
wouldn't give.

Din of this neighborhood's Wi-
Fi names: HONEY-BUMP and
PHONYPONY, FUCKITY, and
FETCHMEAKISS.

Even a din of apologies, the sorriest of
dins.

My American panic that makes me feel like an addict, acres of carp in the river, manic rains…

I was on my hands and knees one night, cleaning barfed-up hot dog from the rug by my son's bed, a din I wept through alone.

Of invisible traps and the pangs of their grip.

Of evidence and the din of forgetting.

All we wanted but never got. All we have and fail to pay attention to.

Din of the hand empty-handed. Of the doom we squeeze into but also the light (we should talk more about it) that returns us to an original shape.

Disentanglement Puzzle

: My daughter solved the disentanglement puzzle; picked a fight with her mother over something someone may or may not have said; filled a jar with wet toilet paper into which she planted sunflower seeds and a handful of hope; put her rats in a handbag; and then, while still in her jammies, skateboarded them around the block on her brother's skateboard, which he was furious about because she didn't even ask.

When she returned, she made a big production of it, unclipped her helmet like it was advanced algebra, kicked off her shoes as if she just crossed a desert.

Finally, she said, *my work is done.*

Folk Song

: Where's the folk song about the pranks that meteorologists play on each other? Where's the folk song cover of "Roxanne"?

Where's the country song about the mediocre scholarship in certain history books?

What about a country song devoted to how worthless credit card payment protection is?

Or a death metal song about a comprehensive approach to sex ed led by qualified professionals?

Where's the ambient industrial trance techno song about the confusing memo your manager sent?

Once, when I was a kid, I wrapped myself in toilet paper and pretended to be a mummy. When my mother got home, she took one look and shook her head. Then we went out for burgers and scratch tickets—

Where's the folk song about that?

Back-To-School Supplies

: Razzed by some dude in the Walmart parking lot for wearing flip-flops (pink) and having my toenails painted (teal).

Summer's hottest song was on a radio somewhere.

I popped a beer, right there in front of the kids, then went and snaked that dude across the parking lot, straight to the last un-bulldozed wetland on the eastside.

I introduced him to a party of invasive red plastic underage drink cups.

I showed him the ducks of no remorse.

Notice the cattails, I said, how they vibrate like the antennae of sunken cars.

It felt like we'd crossed to the other side of summer. A whole dream can have that shape.

My kids, who needed these back-to-school supplies, were learning a valuable lesson like the ones I learned around the bonfires of my hair metal headbanging big pisser youth.

We waited for the swamp uncles to morph up from the sludge.

Eventually I remembered I was almost fifty, and that I've been punched in the head by too many tweets and zombie apocalypse flicks.

When I woke up, I asked my kids, *Who wants ice cream?*

Me! Me! they said, but only if I was buying.

Brother-In-Law

: I was thinking of my brother-in-law for fun.

That time he quit doing acid because he said it gave him acne. That time he ended up at a party in Ypsilanti where they were filming porn in the basement.

He said reading gave him headaches and child support gave him headaches and cigarettes were genetically engineered to his DNA—the list goes on.

My poor wife, she just laughs and shakes her head, but I know she wants to cry.

I went outside to shovel the ton of snow plowed into my drive by the city. When my back hurt and my fingers went numb, I was extremely annoyed. I might've stayed that way awhile, then I remembered my brother-in-law—he's not a bad guy, actually—and immediately felt better.

Eating My Peas

: The parent who invoked whole nations of starving, parentless children—how was I supposed to use that information beyond eating my peas?

What my friend's drunk dad seemed to mean by foreigners were people from anywhere-else... And what my friend's drunk dad seemed to mean by anywhere-else was someplace where goats are sacrificed, and everyone-and-their-brother is either a scam artist or on the hunt for a child-bride.

The monk who feels pleasure when they deny themselves pleasure seems relevant. The key is not to kill even a single bug and to avoid tax penalties.

My friend's drunk dad's drunk friend genuinely seemed to wonder why the kids these days, and everyone-and-their-brother, had these stupid tattoos. The garage we were standing around drinking beer in was filled with machines in desperate need of repair.

The instruction manuals were nowhere in sight.

The Trojan Horse
Appears in New Hampshire

: The motto LIVE FREE OR DIE is
stamped on its ass.

The Red Sox hat someone put on its
head looks comically small.

Whether or not the Trojan Horse is
libertarian or French Canadian is an
argument.

On board, not everyone suffers from
unrequited love.

How shall we discuss history or the
problems of discussing history?

Are there representatives at least
from the Ossipee, Pennacook, and
Winnipesaukee tribes? What enough
will they make of us?

For fun, someone (not wearing a
helmet of course) wheelies in a dirt
bike.

And don't forget the T-shirt of Sarah
Silverman—it expresses somehow
New Hampshire's views on social
taboos.

The not-so-subtle 300-million-year-
old chunk of granite where its heart
should be.

Buckets of clam chowder, maple syrup, Dunkin Donuts—free of tax! But also: mosquitos the size of a baby's head, a purple finch with a lilac in its beak, that New Hampshire accent, all r-lessness and ahs.

I heard the ghost of Robert Frost haunts the head...a weathered muttering thought that wants to scream, *GET OFF MY LAWN...*

The Trojan Horse wheeling through the night, toward the gates of anywhere that is not New Hampshire.

Cancel Culture

: I tried to cancel my credit card. First,
I had to define "cancel" for the guy
on the phone. He said it was from the
Latin. He said it means to obliterate.
He asked me, for security purposes, to
use cancel in a sentence. He put me on
hold with some weird surfer music. He
asked if I was okay. We agreed it was
a tricky question. Relatively speaking,
I said was fine, though I needed a
haircut just then and the news from
top to bottom was nothing but bad. But
the agent said he could totally help me
out. He said canceling my card would
only take a minute, all it required was
a monthly cancellation fee, we could
even handle the paperwork over the
phone. *All we need*, he said, *is your
banking information.* Or, if I preferred,
the monthly cancellation fee could be
charged back to my credit card each
month, simple enough, throughout
the eternity of its canceling.

Phoebe Bourassa

: Phoebe Bourassa drags my ass
through the workout. She shows up
between nightmares with those legs—
oh my god, those legs! She makes me
do sit-ups till I cry.

    Phoebe Bourassa, I say, *I
haven't seen you since junior prom!*

    And she says, *There's a
marathon in you yet, kid!*

    And I say, *Phoebe Bourassa, are
you kidding? Even the news is a virus!*

    And Phoebe says: *You should
see the shit show that was my last gig at
the Parks & Rec!*

    Then she starts in on a million
jumping jacks.

    Forget the world, she says. *Look
at me!*

    Phoebe Bourassa, I say, *I am
looking at you!*

    She whispers in my ear that
this is not a punishment. She makes
me run the hills, with the wind at my
back, until my legs are jelly.

But We Still Have
More Errands to Run

My wife settles the minivan into cruise control. She climbs through the window to the roof and begins to surf.

It's her latest religion.

The road foams. It curls over the front bumper, barrels over other vehicles that wipe out in the shoulder and wash up on the shores of a dying mall.

My wife's hair blows back. She smiles her crazy-smile face. She can't hear me yelling, *But we still have more errands to run!*

To the Lake

Our dinged-up rearview mirror—

The car salesman finally texts and says he'll look into it. There's probably a joke there about hindsight and foresight and useless warranties, but I'm not in the mood.

The frazzled Walmart cashier offers a protection plan for the practically irrelevant portable DVD player my kids will wear out in a season, a situation that remains surprisingly unexamined in the literary canon given how often it occurs.

Soon my mother-in-law will worry the kids will be kidnapped and trafficked the second they're out of sight.

The fog, meanwhile, is full of secrets and offers no apologies.

The mosquitos are just fine trying to suck my blood while I search for a moment of clarity.

Trouble

: What were those kids laughing at?

How much do I owe?

Did the student who speaks fluent Instagram say I should google how to ping Google?

What's changed?

Would you rather have the audio cut out or your cat paw the camera through the critical part of the lesson?

Without electricity, are lessons useless?

Did the CEO have to be a sociopath? Did the president?

Why do I have trouble troubleshooting trouble?

What should we believe?

What do sweatshops, scratch tickets, and cold pizza have in common?

Is the internet a kind of glue?

Is it a church adorned with stained-glass porn and paid ads for free money?

Should I march into the honeysuckle right now?

What time is it?

What were those kids laughing at?

It's complicated...

Clouds

: Clouds like junk mail.

Clouds like the eight hours a day, five days a week, fifty weeks a year, thirty years and counting I've had to hustle for my cake.

Clouds that refuse to help my kids out with their homework, or maybe they weren't paying attention.

Clouds not like Molotov cocktails, but there was lightning.

Clouds like that dude in the chicken suit smoking a cigarette in the Kwik Trip parking lot.

Clouds with or without pronouns. Clouds that vanish like a student loan should.

Clouds like one of everything. Clouds like an absence of clouds.

Clouds that dare you to get some sleep or eat a cricket.

That dare you to walk into a field and let the last honeybees dance on your face.

Yellow Rain Slicker

: The bay was flat and still; that seemed
to be its point.

The news seemed less important than
the reality of my kids wondering
what's for breakfast and my therapist
saying just listen.

It's possible...the hummingbirds that
divebombed the feeder...the yellow
rain slicker hung by the door...it's
possible these were not metaphors for
beauty or anything.

Otherwise, I felt softer and calm, at
large and alone, unconcerned as the
bay confided nothing.

It did not go viral as it reflected the
sky.

It was not a church.

It just felt that way when I held my
breath and finally jumped in.

Acknowledgments

Thanks to the journals where the following poems first appeared, sometimes in a slightly different form or with a different title.

The Cafe Review: "Yellow Rain Slicker"
Defunct: "Worst Punk Band" and "Rubber Chicken"
South Carolina Review: "I, Too, Have Been Unfaithful"
Southern Indiana Review: "Back-To-School Supplies"
Third Coast: "Bigger Wave"
Tupelo Quarterly: "This Guy from Turkey"

A version of "Folk Song" appeared in *Ope!*, an anthology published by the Wisconsin Institute for Creative Writing.

"Credit Card" appears in *Level Land: Poems for and about the I35 Corridor* (Lamar University Literary Press).

To my "what if?" brothers: Josh Bell, Ron Mitchell, Mike Theune, and Jake Penner.

Special thanks for the time and space to Shake Rag Alley, Madison College, and the Bethany Arts Center.

To Erika Meitner and Sandra Simonds for the invaluable feedback on early drafts of this book. *Doom Scroll* would not exist without you.

To Mary Biddinger and The University of Akron Press for the continued support.

To Julie Larson-Guenette, for love and patience.

For August and Jozi...

Matthew Guenette grew up in New Hampshire. He earned
an MA in English from the University of New Hampshire
and an MFA in creative writing from Southern Illinois
University. He is the author of three previous poetry col-
lections, including *Vasectomania* (2017), *American Busboy*
(2011), and *Sudden Anthem* (2008). He lives in Madison,
WI, with his wife, their two children, and a twenty-pound
cat named Butternut.